From the Passenger Window

Xtina Marie

Dedication:

I write about my life and the things that move me. The beautiful and the devastating. As with the majority of my poetry, you can find more than just pieces of me, but a look behind the curtain as to what makes me tick. So for that— for giving me something to write about, I would like to dedicate this book to all of the people in my life who've inspired my verse, whether they be my angels, or my demons. ♥

Acknowledgements:

As always, I'd like to thank Luke Spooner for the amazing artwork on the cover. I give him a brief idea of what I am looking for, and he delivers exactly the perfect image!

Thank you so much to Denise Jury who is still catching my boo-boos all these years later. She has a way of seeing what my eyes can't.

Thank you to Rosemary O'Brien who keeps setting the poetry bar higher and higher!

A big thank you to James Longmore, who would love to read some rhyming poetry, if he is forced to read any at all, (even though I am still pretty taken with free verse) yet he keeps agreeing to publish the next book!

Thank you to all of my readers, all 5 of you! 😄 I'd say you keep me going, but truth be told, I write to quiet the darkness, and I don't care to thank it again.

Thank you to my wonderful husband who quelled some of my demons. He makes it safe for me to visit them in my memories from time to time, giving me inspiration for my poetry.

Contents:

You may not find a path, but you will find a way.
-Tom Wolfe

Fly
For Shawn

The sky resembles the color
of fresh bruises
and I anguish over lost time,
scrolling through years
that feel like minutes or decades
depending on the day…

nonsensical moments
plague my memory;

a dark-haired baby
learning to crawl
in the winter on threadbare carpets
and drafty Wisconsin houses…

a precocious little boy

with a steady barrage
of seemingly endless chatter
to fill the silence
and brooding eyes
that fail to hide an old soul…

a sensitive teen
and first heartbreaks
that broke me a little inside
when all I could do was cry silently,
no longer able
to fix every boo-boo

a wonderfully unique man
I've not yet met
and the bittersweet knowledge
that it's almost time
to watch you fly

Her Only Friend at 3 a.m.

To my wild child

She wears
sadness
like a sweatshirt
drab, black
and heavy,
shapeless
but suffocating

it's familiar
yes, achingly so
and at 3 a.m.
her sadness
is her only
confidant
so she embraces
the despair

content with
how natural
and easy it is
allowing
the darkness
to envelope her

happiness
is
now
her
enemy

Anything but Binding

I sleep
in your chains
cold and weighty
against
warm flesh

and it's…
anything
but binding

it's…

calming
and soothing
protective
and claiming

a constant reminder
that I am
not only yours

but…

loved
needed
wanted
secure

for another
night

i draw hearts

i draw hearts
in the sand
during summer
with bare toes,
nails painted pink
or red
maybe purple,
always looking
to find
romance
in whatever
surrounds me;
his slow smile
and that twinkle
he gets
in his eyes
when he laughs

i draw hearts
in the frost
of car windows
during winter
with frozen fingertips,
nails painted maroon
or pearl white,
my heart warmed
by the romance
all around me,
his husky breath
at my ear
whispering
sweet nothings
sending shivers
down my spine
and thrills
to my core

i draw hearts

South Side of Heaven

Miss you, Robbie

she was imperfect,
unruly, and a little
crazy at times
but always with
the best of
intentions,
she was quick
to tell you...
she'd help raise
a little hell
while straightening
her halo
and couldn't resist
cussing from
the last pew in church...
I still miss her laugh

and the way she sang
that Eagles' song
when she was
a little tipsy
but I'm sure
I'll see her again
even if it's
on the south side
of Heaven

Winter's Eyes

stealing shivers
from winter's eyes
demand nothing
of the sun
and its
withered flowers

Toxic Words

Why do we hurt
the ones we love
with poison dripping
vile words
we'd not say
in polite company?

I ponder
sitting silent,
the warm tears
dried to
pale cheeks,
my heart bruised
by the one
promising to
love me most

I wonder
if my answer
awaits
between
cold sheets
in the bed
we'll share
after suffering
awkwardly
through

a miserable evening
because
we forget
toxic words
aren't easily
forgotten

Late night
tears
bring morning
clarity

A Stranger

You look different
to me today,
I think it was
something
you said…
or maybe that tone
in your voice
when you looked at me
as if you didn't
know me anymore
but really it was you
who'd turned into
a stranger

Winter's Ghost

strangled
by the
destruction
of life
with it's
strings and vines
and loud fitting
twisted hopes
that pirouette away,
silenced by
winter's ghost
and cremated moments
nonetheless

Between

thrill me
with your
ghosts and spirits,
the specters too
on the cool nights
when the fog rolls in
during those months
between—
before spring bears
new wildflowers
as if in offering
to the frigid
winter gods

Xtina Marie

But Mostly

i dream of
tents and stars,
campfires and body heat
i dream of seeing
the world
through the eyes
of a gypsy
and the heart
of a child...
i dream of hitchhiking
and listening to
stories told by
travelers
passing through
but mostly
i dream of you

These Darker Selves

the photograph...
your shadow,
impossibly common,
the old magic—
a capture we
recognize...
no effort to reveal
these darker selves
alone

Winter waves
goodbye
with uncontrolled fury
and wind howling
it's displeasure

The Unfolding Spring

shouting
almost joyous
deep into
the winter trees
with their still skies
and treacherous streets
completely shadows
the unfolding spring

Tangled

Often
the words
I write
are still
tangled
up in you
because
a part of me
refuses to
let you go

Unravel

unravel
the sweet
pain
of broken
poetry,
helplessly
exposed
with beautiful
wounds
and phrases
purposefully
rearranged by
healing scars

his beating heart
told her
no other
time or place
existed

Nothing United

Stand up
for what
you believe in…
but only if
you believe
the same as me.

There can be
no middle ground and
no arguing sides,
it's my way
or the highway

And I will get
all my friends
to bully and mock you,
drag your name

through mud
if you go against
what I believe

Because my way
is the right way,
the only way…
and I will
keep spewing
hate and
disharmony
that the media
perpetuates
until there is
nothing
United
about our states
anymore

Long Dead Poets

long dead poets
still spilling
centuries old blood,
their whispers
and cries
floating silently
from within
thin yellowed pages
on musty
bookshelves
imbued with
cryptic stanzas and
ominous lines,
painful secrets
hidden between
lyrical words
daring us to join in

and bleed along
one last time

Flames of Romance

fire;
passion
dancing
with flames
of romance
on lonely nights
like fierce
poetry,
dreamy and seeking
a home
in perfect
little poems

I'm High

the smell
of his shirt
intoxicates me
and I inhale
a deep breath
of him,
holding it in
as I would
a drug,
letting it flow
around me
and through me
til I can feel him
in every inch
of my being
and I'm high
on the fragrance

of his love
once more

The Ink of Poems

escape
in the ink
of poems
crafted by
whispering kisses
and quiet nights

Adapting

like an
animal;
i survive,
i learn
to adapt

drinking
and music,
alone and
absorbed
in thoughts

Heavenly

I'm no
angel
but when
you look at me
from across
a room,
those eyes
following
every move
I make,
I feel
heavenly

I Dream of Summer

I dream of summer
and warm grass
between bare toes,
the squeals of
neighborhood children
playing in the street
and dogs barking...

I dream of summer
and quiet evenings
on the porch swing,
your arm around
my shoulders
while the sun dips down
and out of sight
and the insects come out
to serenade us

I dream of summer
and sweltering nights
between cotton sheets,
your kisses blazing
a scorching trail
down my fevered body
and the slow, steady pound
of rain on the window

I dream of summer

She can
light up a room
on fire

Sandcastles

years crashing
like relentless dreams
silent and impossible
and sometimes
the sounds
we *do* hear
are just
sandcastles
drowning
in the waves

When He Was Drinking

He always
liked me better
when he was
drinking;
the warm
alcohol buzz
bubbling
through his
veins,
when he could
forget
all the miles
between us
and the sad truth
that he'd
never know
the soft touch

of my hand
in his
or the smell
of my perfume..

I always
liked him better
when he was
drinking;
his normally
all-business voice
warm and relaxed
by the whiskey,
when I could
close my eyes
and feel his
calloused fingers
griping mine,
or smell
his cologne;
spicy yet comforting
washing over me

Snowflakes Remember

bitter words tangle,
finding
the spring fields
blooming with
nourishing smiles...
and love
beneath the
branches
of winter
snowflakes
remember

Fraud

I'm a fraud
a fake
not who you think
and if you
ran into me
at a party...
well
you wouldn't--
I wouldn't be
invited
or if I was
I'd be the girl
hiding
near the exit
hoping no one
notices
with my

caught-in-the-headlights
look in my eyes
petrified
heart erratic
and roaring in my ears
icy sweat
trickling down
the small
of my back
causing my shirt
to cling uncomfortably
and feel like
a pretty pale rose
prison,
a jail
and my fear
is the jailor
my hands
cuffed figuratively
tight, restrictive
and I can't reach
behind me
 to yank at the
soft fabric
wet and clammy
plastered to my back
so I just stand there
averting my eyes
hoping no one
notices

that I am
not what you think
I am
a fraud

Prettier
when
I
bleed

Danger

You're the danger
of driving
way too fast
on country roads
in the rain
windows down
radio blaring…
it's not *if*
I lose control
but *when*…
and I'm aware
the crash will
irrevocably alter

every

last

thing

yet I can't help
but to
close my eyes
and pray the impact
doesn't kill us all

Dream Impossibilities

Dream impossibilities
like waves crashing
beside picnics
at sunset,
cherry-red skirts
in the summer heat
rising like a balloon
on the boardwalk,
and poetry
forever written
at midnight
full of shiny
bouquets of love

Xtina Marie

the pages are
blank
the readers
appear
to be
dozing off

Lonely Miss

the bitter
ache
remains...
lonely miss
left
weeping
each year
till every
concealed
pain is
remembered

I Cannot See

true–
in the middle
of the night
we wander the
shadowless air,
eyes closed
with invisible threads
glistening quietly...
i cannot see
beyond it

this world,
a theater of
good and evil
the center of everything
the garden of dust

Candy Apples

gazing at
brilliant red skies,
temptation
blossoms wicked
like the taste
of a candy apple,
all sweetness and
satisfying

So Very Something

It's the quiet
of 2 a.m.
that I crave…
the stillness,
the calm,
the tranquility
of the moon
and the stars
and the
conversations
they have
that I lazily
eavesdrop upon
while gazing
into the blackness,
into the void

hoping for a
glimpse
of the nothing
that is so very
something
and I yearn
to understand
the intricate
language
being whispered
into the darkness

The Words

Some days
I long
to write—
but words
escape me
no matter
how hard
I try
to reach
for them,
desiring to
purge myself
from some
unseen
demon
that's come
to call

yet again
but I'm not able
to see his face,
for he hides
his identity—
I'm sure
to prevent me
from
casting him
back
to the hell
in which he
came from,
forcing me
to live in agony
day after day,
tormenting
my mind
with the silence
that comes
from the
inability
to cleanse
the palate
of my soul
by releasing
the words--
always the words
--back into
the void,

into the abyss
into the emptiness
so that I can
again,
find the
peace
the quiet
the tranquility
I seek

Sanctuary

Do you think
this is what
it's like,
to be alive
but not living?
To see your hair
lift in a breeze
you can never feel
upon your skin?
Or hear the sounds
from a world
outside your window
that you'll never touch?
The cars speeding by
impatient to get to
a place you'll never visit,
their dwellings filled with

people you'll never greet?

This immaculately sterile room
your mind's created
to protect you
from some travesty
in your past
you've buried deep
and refuse to deal with
is not the sanctuary
you intended it to be,
but a prison with no parole
and the only jailer
is yourself,
yet you refuse
to insert the key

So, pull up the chair
and gaze down
at the street below

to get a better view
of the life you
could be living
if only,

you could remember
how to live it

On the Rocks

Never again,
she says
naked,
day drinking
a daiquiri
in bed,
the arm of a
mercurial man,
asleep
remains warm
around her—
but nothing
means love like
a smooth Margarita
on the rocks
at four in the morning

*life
surprised me...
always
a struggle,
never giving...
a strange way
and perfectly
matter-of-fact*

Beautiful Poetic Longing

fingertips whisper
beautiful poetic
longing
over
warm flesh
oft
sizzling passion

Perfection

summer air
soft like that
perfect rose
and that
golden
setting sun...
a sweet wind
stirring trees
and the whirring
of cicadas outside...

perfection

A legend

you could only
see her
at twilight
as the sun
was setting
but not quite
nighttime
just yet,
wearing a long
white dress,
the bottom
dirty and in
tatters,
walking alone,
her dark hair
billowing behind her...

they say
it was tragic;
the crash
that ended
the lives
of her loved ones
as well as hers
that fateful night
decades ago...

they say
she's haunted
this road
since then
and teens
giggle nervously
while eying
what lies
in front of them
hoping the legend

is just that...
a legend

i've known loss
and can feel
her anguish
long before
i catch
a glimpse
of white
in the distance

and i mourn
with her

Spring in Tennessee

Spring
in Tennessee
means
the top down,
flying over
twisty
backroads
with the music
blaring
something funky,
arms out
to catch the breeze,
the freedom
so accessible
'til it seeps
through splayed
fingers

reminding us
just how fleeting
this life is

so make sure

you live it

*tomorrow's
hopes and dreams,
become
moments gone
either
joys or sorrows*

Where the Tattered Ruins of My Heart Weep

i hurt...
mental pain,
--agony--
is filled with
sweet fragile
darkness,
an aching void
where the
tattered ruins
of my heart
weep

Paranoia

they were
watching me…
with their
piercing eyes,
eyes that stared
directly
into my soul,
judging me
condemning me
even talking
about me
when I couldn't
see them,
when I was
just out of sight
and I could
no longer

hear them,
but I knew…
I knew it in
the way they
glanced away
when I entered
a room
when I tried
desperately
to make
eye contact
or make any
connection
at all
and I start
to scream out
in frustration,
in hysteria
but still
they pay me

no mind at all
until I am
just a sobbing
mess of nerves
on the ground
frantically praying
the eyes,
those piercing eyes
that stare directly
into my soul
leave me be

Honestly

honestly
I know
the sweetness
of your kiss
and the
wonderful
warmth
your lips
hold
as they
gently part

the words
are gone;
what doesn't say
hides behind
the hush

Just Yesterday

over the years
i've watched your beard
go from chestnut brown
to nearly all white
and the little crinkle
between your brows deepen...

middle age
looks good on you,
distinguished and confident
and when you
wink at me like that
I'm a school girl again
pressing my leg
against yours
in that little red truck,

flirting, unashamed
trying to catch your eye
not realizing
i'd always had...

so long ago
yet it seems like
just yesterday
and I wonder when today

will seem like

just yesterday

We've Never Been Whole

Silent,
like deep waters
with only
the sound
of blood
rushing through
my veins
and the pounding
in my head
I lie here
unmoving,
barely a breath
I take
as the darkness
creeps into
my thoughts,

into my soul
and I am mournful
that you cannot
see into the
mirror of my eyes
into your own
darkness
to know that

we've never
been whole

Poetry of Today

Bathe darkness
from dewy skin
and cleanse together
with tomorrow's passion
a forever kiss
heightened by
the poetry of today

Completely and Utterly Be

regretting
our time
is not
the real problem…
those other versions,
those lives are
happening…
we can't feel
every pleasure,
we just have to
completely and utterly
be

If Only for the Night

I visit with
fireflies
on warm
summer evenings,
the dewy grass
cool and sticky
on the backs
of my thighs …
I watch as they
leisurely flit
from here to there
as if they've
no real
destination,
just seemingly
stopping

at random spots
to converse
with the flowers,
and I envy
the secrets
they share,
wishing to be
included
in their private
moments
if only
for the night

The Loneliness

Dreaming;
I possibly
just didn't like
the loneliness,
the loss of
myself,
the loss
of who
I had been

Make it a Good One

There is a story in her eyes
that she's reluctant
to share…

a story of pain
and years of distrust
she's endured
at the hands
of someone
meant to protect her

but instead of
lashing out in
retribution

she realizes
the world is full

of injustices
heartaches
ugliness

and that
she's the only one
controlling
how the rest of her life
will be shaped

and she's determined

to make it a good one

His Touch was a Whisper

Tempted,
I brushed
his fingers--
flirted,
his touch
was a whisper
spreading
a complicated
knot of emotion

A Swirling Storm

there's nothing like a
swirling storm
exploding
inside a
sensual heart
to make
everything
fabulous

No Real Talent

There are times
when the words
fail me
and the blinding white
of the computer screen
mocks me
telling me
I am nothing,
I possess no
real talent
and I begin
to believe

Strangers Leftover

I've been
thinking
about you…
strangers leftover
from the fire—
only these
brief moments
dwelling here

Don't Shoot

It's the wrong time—
but was there ever
a *right* time
for somebody new,
for you, for us
for the little bit
of comfort
we let ourselves
believe was
love?

yet,
you pulled me
through
when life was
determined
to trample me alive

and spit me out
gasping for air
and begging to be
loosened from the
pain and agony
I had mistakenly thought
I'd grown accustomed

This is not
what I do
and you were never
a game
despite the fact
you now feel played
so, give my gun away
but don't shoot…

it's loaded

bound to you
through
invisible threads...
I call
to you

He's Back

The demon is back…
he lay dormant,
quiet and still
waiting for me
to forget
the horror,
the nightmare
I was forced
to endure,
biding his time
hoping the memories
of him had faded
and I was
completely unaware
he'd been
silently stalking
everything I hold dear

everything I cherished
until his sharp teeth
took hold of

everything

and

devoured

it

whole

There's Nothing

shattered
broken…
the hurt
consumes,
crawling up
my aching body
with skeletal fingers
wanting to wrap soundly
around my swollen
and parched throat

hot salty tears
track soundlessly
down flushed cheeks
trying to expel
the pain

—the absolutely
soul wrenching pain—
that has engulfed me

I clutch
at the pain,
sure there must be
a wound
or blood,
something that could
explain away
the source
of this agony

but there's nothing

The Rotting Solitude

silence—
merely cracks
of dread engraved
from my memory,
stumbling endlessly
on decaying voices
beyond the echo…
and only the rotting solitude
will come to wake me

The Next Destination

Death never looked
quite as fetching
as it did every
November,
in Tennessee;
the leaves
scattered about
slick roads
all weathered
and colorful,
forlorn, somber
saying goodbye
to the short life
they enjoyed
before returning
to the cold earth below…

and I watch them
from out of
the passenger window
crunching under tires
to float soundlessly
behind us
as we speed to
our next destination…

and I wonder
do the leaves
ever wish
they had taken
the scenic route,
a slower path
to their
next destination
and the cold earth below

Rain Puddle

Big city lights
come alive
at night
in the winter,
illuminated with
a welcoming warmth
despite walking down
wet streets
alone but never
lonely
free and floating
through life
one rain puddle
at a time

His Words Could Not

He kissed me
with anger
and all of
the passion
he'd kept
inside,
hidden
and I was
never too sure
if he loved me
or hated me
as our lips
and mouths
came together
in animalistic
mating
but I could
not deny
the kiss
said everything
his words
could not

Autumn Bleeds

Autumn bleeds
into the
skeletal remains
of winter,
it's cadaverous
fingers
reaching out
to take me
by the hand,
inviting me
into the darkness,
the bleak night
engulfing
all the warmth
and life
that Summer
had fooled us

into believing
would never end

Favorite Bad Decision

He liked to
tell me
I'd always be
his favorite
bad decision
and to
give him
a call
should I have
an itch
I just
couldn't
quite scratch,
but truth
be told
it was probably
the toxic addicted

routine
we sometimes
missed –
the fights
at 2 a.m.
ensuring we'd be
blurry eyed and
annoyed
the next day,
and the angry
make-up sex
a week later
where we
punished
each other
with bruises and
scratches
in the name
of love…
but really,

we were just
2 lonely souls
looking for
someone
to blame
when shit
went bad,
and I
push *end*
on my cell
before
the call
connects
because
you'll always be
my favorite
bad decision
as well

I May Read These Words

I write
so that
when
I am old
and I've
forgotten
the smell
of your
favorite
old t-shirt,
I may read
these words
and be
reminded
just how
intoxicating
you are

to me

Christmas with You

For Christian

I still
remember
our first
December
together
in the
Florida heat,
walking on
the beach
Christmas day,
the sand warm
and soothing
on frost bit
New York toes
hoping to thaw

but I'll
always prefer
to watch
the lazy
snowflakes
dance
and twirl
in the wind
while we
snuggle close
on the couch
with my fuzzy socks
by the light of
the Christmas tree
in the Tennessee
mountains

You Feel it Too

I still
talk to you
in my head
and I can still
hold you
in my dreams

but when I wake

your warm body
poofs
dissipates
and I am left
surrounded by
cold air and longing

and the
only thing
that remains
is the comfort
that

you feel it too

A Warmth I've Never Felt

Can you hear it?

The quiet beauty
of winter
as it muffles
the day-to-day
chaos with
calming tranquility
and freezing hope

stinging tears
fall from
a white sky
to land upon
the naked road,
concealing
ugly imperfections

and turmoil

blanketing them
with soft serenity
and conforming
the mundane
into something
majestic and magical
breathtaking even—

and for a short time
I am transported
to a wonderland
of shivering
expectations

and a warmth
I've never felt
in Summer

Garland Hopes & Tinsel Dreams

I'll never
outgrow
my love
for Christmas
and the awe
of garland hopes
and tinsel dreams

snowflakes
fluttering
from frigid
lashes
drift soundlessly
to blanket the earth--
the day-to-day hustle
masquerading
as sweet tranquility

the whole
world
just pauses
as if it were
suspended
in a snow globe
or Kinkade painting
and we celebrate
love, family
kindness, beauty
never forgetting
our Savior's birth

the angels sigh
and wish
for one moment
to be human
and experience
the most wonderful
time of the year
as we wait for Santa,
sitting under
the colorful lights
of the tree
our hearts full
of garland hope
and tinsel dreams

How They Fluttered

If I've ever
loved you,
if my heart
has ever
galloped
in my chest
to the mention
of your name,
or my cheeks
flushed
at the sound
of your voice—

understand…

you still
wander

through my
mind
when I
least expect it
and I recall
the butterflies
and how they
fluttered
for you
like
wild birds
startled
by a loud noise
flapping their
untamed wings…

and for a moment

time stands still
as if my heart

still beat
for
only you

Fluttering Verses

artists possibly
blossom
in the morning
with the birds
and coffee
and escape reality
through journals
or opened windows
accompanied by
the sun's rays
and dream of
fluttering verses
that rhyme like
leaves

What You Didn't Say

The silence
was awkward
and loud,
echoing in the
nothingness,
stretching out
making the minutes
feel like hours
as I lie
next to you
in bed,
sleep evading,
while an
endless night
loomed,
and yet still
what you didn't say

hurt worst of all

The Chemicals

...and wept
anything good
had left

i had quit
the chemicals
that made me ill

so beautiful,
a true beauty

i was most likely
still in love

No One But Each Other

We liked to
make a
splash
wherever
we went,
so hellbent
on showing
the world
how eccentric
we could be
because really
we were
the only people
in our
little world

we needed
no one
but
each other

Savage Dead

leave the
rot
at the
bottom,
the cracked
don't mend…
go after
that place
stuffed with
savage dead,
who drifts
patiently
and destroys
necessity

Romance-Dipped Dreams

poetry
can excite
desires
from moaning lips
and loosen
thighs
like
romance-dipped
dreams

No One Noticed

Something broke
last night
while we were
too busy
being right,
too busy
being hurt,
too busy
being indignant
to notice
the shattered pieces
of what once was
lying brokenly
on the floor
no longer resembling
the beautiful spectacle
it had been

Something broke
in the middle of
the raised voices
and the hot tears,
but no one noticed
until it was too late
and we weren't sure
where to find
all the pieces…

Had they slid
under the bed,
blown under the
crack in the door,
or perhaps in between
the cushions
of the couch?

Something broke
and it was
painfully obvious
that, while we could
apologize and
say sorry
over and over again,
some of the
shattered pieces
would never
rightly fit
where they once were

and the worst part was

no one noticed

Crumbled Mess

reaching for
answers
in the
crumbled mess
of a
kingdom
like taking
milk
out of the cup
the baby
spills

Useless Stuff

Crazy,
like useless stuff
we keep
forgetting...
memories
fuel memories;
pictures of
ten thousand
fires
while it burns
exactly the
same

One Last Kiss

She kissed him
with barbed wire
lipstick,
bright red
and cunning,
stealing
the breath
he was breathing
with a
sweet smile
that hid
sharp pointy
teeth
waiting
to tear into
his heart

and leave him
lying in a
heap on the
cold floor
while he begged
for the mercy
he knew
she'd not
grant him
and yet,
yet
he knew
when the end
was near
and handed her
the knife
in the hopes of
one last
kiss

In the Silence

In the
silence
I can still
hear you
even after
years have
passed
turning lovers
into strangers

and while
my mind
realizes
we've moved on

my heart
remembers

The Same Things

I've been
a liar
a thief
a convict
a cheat
an addict
a drunk

and all of
those things
you've thought
about me

are true

because

they're
the same things

I think about me
too

Where I was Always Meant to Be

You smelled like
virility and comfort
and your mouth
tasted
of home

the years we'd
wasted
melted into
the hotel
mattress
with the
firm press
of your
body
against mine

and I knew
your arms
were where
I was always

meant
to
be

He Will Always Rot

I've always
wanted
the ache,
the constant
reminder
of betrayal
to remember
he will
always
rot
inside
of me

House of Sadness

In this house
of sadness
we had been
friends
for many years

a wild sickness
of the heart
forced the
desire
to believe in
decaying walls
and quiet dreams

Don't Get Used to This

Understand
holding my hand
burns a little

I get restless
I squirm

I trust nostalgia
because
memories
are real

Don't get used
to this
it's ending soon

Feigned Worth

Sobriety
offers
permanent
discomfort
and feigned
worth,
an approval
that's irrelevant
and forced

Almost Worth It

Your pursed lips
showed too much,
especially for me
with my
forced smiles
and discomfort

irrelevant
and always
will be
but
you're almost
worth it

pain goes
deep
gnawing scary
little aches

Wild, Nonetheless

the balloon
drifted
slowly on
all night

it wasn't
black wings
but it was
wild
nonetheless

Always Wild

love's
intricate
kisses
like whispers
caught
in broken
spider webs
forgotten

always wild

Our Love is Easy

Love
should be
easy

lying on
the couch
in our underwear
watching
Beavis and Butt-head
to combat
a rough
workday

enjoying
the silence
while we read
in bed

at night
not pressured
to think of
something to say

getting up
to make dinner
and hearing
the opening strands
of that Rembrandts song
from the
living room tv
because you know
I like to watch
Friends
while I cook

reaching out to you
in the middle

of the night
if I've had
a bad dream,
because you are
my refuge,
my safety,
my comfort

even on the
hard days
our love
is easy

Spring's Footprints

he always said
his birthday
was in May
even though
he's really
a December baby
and I remember
holding the warm can
of *OV Splits*
up to his
shapely, talented mouth
as the tattoo gun
whirled against
his upper arm
and the warm beer
spilled down

his chin,
both of us
laughing
and a little buzzed

I can still
smell
youthful excitement
and young love
when the
opening notes
of that *Def Leppard* song
come on
the radio
and I'm transported
to that day in May
as we sang *Happy Birthday*
in the warmth
of a New York
spring

knowing full well

he wouldn't be
a year older
till snow covered
spring's footprints
and the tattoo
was no longer
fresh and new

Xtina Marie

I Break My Own Heart

I'm a poet…

sometimes
I break
my own
heart
hoping
my words
help me

when
the devastation
of my
fiction
becomes
reality

Kentucky Nights

Kentucky nights
in the spring
roll over me
like a warm wave
crashing gently
to baptize me
in honeysuckle
and contentment
as we get lost
on twisting
backroads,
green leaves
dancing in the
rearview mirror
much as my

hair dances
across my face
while the
radio blares
some 80s hair band
and I honestly
cannot imagine
that anything
could be

better

than

this

Summer's Hello

It's the perfect day
to hunt for
four leaf clovers
in the
backyard
lying on
sunbaked grass
tickling the
backside of
our legs

let's play
I spy
with the
fluffy white clouds
to the music

of the
neighborhood kids
riding bikes
in the road
and the harmonizing dogs
barking at every
movement

pretend for
a moment
we don't have
nine to fives
and laundry to fold,
dishes to do
and bills to pay

instead
watch the sun
dip low
as the fireflies dance

and the smell

of hotdogs
on the grill
season the air
with anticipation
of Summer's hello
cheerfully waving
as Spring finally
packs her bags
and bids us all
farewell

Xtina Marie

The Heat of June

lilies
this morn'
and
the heat
of June
wrap around
my youth
and
the petals are
tendrils
of my hair
–suddenly–
I'm a
jewel

Poetry

Songs about
walks
in the woods
with a stranger
and the
beauty
of butterflies

the feeling
of floating
in love
as a sunset
stills
your heartbeat

poetry

set to
the music
of life

Someday
For Jen

I'm not sure
she'll ever know
how much
I really
love her
because
sometimes
I'm so
terribly
bad at
showing it

I forget to ask
how she's doing
and if she's

happy,
how the kids are
and does the
hubby still
treat her well

but I promise to call
someday soon
we'll catch up then

life
has this way
of getting busy,
—moving so fast—
and before
I know it
it's been;
6 months
a year

longer

and I just hope
she knows
when someone
asks about
my best friend
it's always her
and I treasure
every memory
we've ever
shared

Supernatural marathons
and awkward
family dinners
at the
Chinese buffet…
the time
we sped off

in the car
to chase a
cheating boyfriend…
and I'm sure
illegal substances
were involved
the night
we swear we heard
the ghost bird

oh, to be able
to create
more memories
as we
grow older

and maybe
we will
someday

somedays
I wish

someday

was here

Makes You Wonder

I don't know
anymore
I might
be too
old

photographs
become
beautiful
stories

every moment
makes
you wonder
are we
infinite?

We Shall Flower

We are alive…

slowly
slowly

we shall
flower

From the Passenger Window

There's something
exhilarating
about
driving fast
through the
mountains,
top down,
hair whipping
across your face;
stinging

and I am
content
next to you,
the passenger princess,
watching the world
fly by,

too fast sometimes
to even bring
into focus
what I am seeing
before
it's gone again

one hand
trying to
keep loose strands
of my hair
at bay
the other
closed over yours
on the gear shift,
my heart full
—so damn full—
of this life,
this love
this moment

with you

I smile
at you
and you give me
that wink
(the one
that makes me
clench my thighs
tight together)
before I turn back
to my favorite view
from the
passenger window

About the Author

The Short Version:
Book Publisher, Poet, Podcaster, Writer,
Mom, Bibliophile…

The Accidental Poet:

Xtina Marie is an avid horror and fiction genre reader, who became a blogger; who became a published poet; who became an editor; who now is a book publisher and CEO of Hell Bound Books Publishing with her co-host on The Panic Room Radio Show, James H. Longmore.

Her first book of poetry, Dark Musings has received outstanding reviews. It is likely Xtina was born to this calling. Writing elaborate twisted tales to entertain her classmates in middle school would later lead Xtina to use her poetry as a private emotional outlet in adult life—words she was hesitant to share publicly—but the more she shared, the more accolades her writing received.

She has two additional poetic narrative editions, Light Musings and Darkest Sunlight, a combination of both light and dark poetry. In 2018, Xtina fell in love with free verse, and began writing Without the Confines of My Rhymes, which was released in 2019. In 2020 she released her follow up free verse book, Immortalize Me.

Xtina has contributed works to the following:
Suite 269 by Christine Zolendz
Busted Lip: An Anthology
Monsters of Metal: An Anthology
The Intermission, Gore Carnival Book 2
A Lovely Darkness: Poetry with Heart
Black Candy: A Halloween Anthology of Horror
Collected Christmas Horror Shorts by Kevin J. Kennedy
Slashing Through the Snow: A Christmas Horror Anthology
Depraved Desires: Volume 1
Beautiful Tragedies
Damsels of Distress
Pieces of Us: A Collection of Flash Fiction, Short Stories, and Poetry
Subliminal Messages: A Collection of Poetry, Prose, and Quotes
Leaves of the Poet Tree by Andrew Aitken
Apocalypse of the Heart by Leah Negron and friends
Poetry Friends in Rhythm & Rhyme by Leah Negron
Graveyard Girls by Gerri R. Gray
Further Within Darkness & Light: A Collection of Poetry by Paul B Morris
The Light Shines Through: Anthology of Poetry

Paper Cuts

Other titles by Xtina:
Light Musings
Darkest Sunlight
Without the Confines of My Rhymes
Immortalize Me
Wild, Imperfect & Messy
Where the Dirt Road Leads

Xtina resides in the beautiful state of Tennessee, with her family, four yapping ankle biters and 4 ball pythons.

You can find Xtina:
http://www.hellboundbookspublishing.com/index.html
https://www.facebook.com/XtinaMarie4031/
https://www.facebook.com/ThePanicRoomRadioShow/
https://www.amazon.com/Xtina-Marie/e/B01E1QNI3O?ref=sr_ntt_srch_lnk_1&qid=1589142288&sr=8-1

OTHER POETRY FROM HELLBOUND BOOKS
www.hellboundbookspublishing.com

Immortalize Me

"Immortalize Me is raw, beautiful, and poignant. This subtle yet hypnotic dance between darkness and light is a poetry lover's delight!"

- USA Today Bestselling Author, K Webster

With a style echoing the late Audre Lorde, Xtina Marie's newest poetry collection Immortalize Me - with its striking imagery and layered free-verse simplicity - reveals a provocative, candid look at Xtina's story told in fragments - intimate snapshots of moments of submission and raw passion, nostalgia and drifting daydreams, anguish and quiet contemplation. All in all, a bold, haunting, bittersweet collection.

"As lyrical as song and as faceted as a diamond, Xtina Marie's latest collection is a riot of imagery and emotion that pushes buttons and boundaries alike. IMMORTALIZE ME does just what it says - her words will linger in your blood long after the last page has been read."

- Alistair Cross, author of The Book of Strange Persuasions and the Vampires of Crimson Cove series

"Xtina Marie's words punch you in the gut, hit you in the feels, and put you in her past in a way that forces you to confront your own. She wields a pen the way witches wave wands... purely magic."

From the Passenger Window

- Carver Pike (horror and dark fantasy author)

<u>Without the Confines of my Rhymes</u>

Poetry is a beautiful thing, illustrating thoughts and emotions with concise, well-chosen words. A lot of poetry rhymes, adding additional flavor to the words, giving them a sense of rhythm, of flow

But what happens when you take away the rhyming, when you cast off the forms of convention and good sense?

Then the interesting things begin to come out. When the next line doesn't need to rhyme, anything can come next. As it is within the poems themselves, so it is with this book in its entirety.

Casting off the rhyming styles she used before, Xtina Marie embarks on a journey of emotional ups and downs, reflecting on love, loss, children and art.

So settle in, put on your wine-colored glasses, and take a trip without the confines of rhymes.

<u>Darkest Sunlight</u>

"The heart was made to be broken."
- *Oscar Wilde*

To allow your heart to soar, you must risk the depths. Darkest Sunlight is the third poetic narrative from Xtina Marie. In this journey, readers will begin in the darkest of places yet revealed to us by this critically acclaimed poet, only to then find themselves thrust into the brightness of love before their eyes and minds can fully adjust.

It is this shocking contrast which best conveys what it is to love, lose, and love again.

In Dark Musings, Xtina explored sadness. In Light Musings, she explored the intricacies of a loving heart. In Darkest Sunlight, Xtina Marie compares the opposite ends of the spectrum, and in doing so, she found a place darker than black.

__Dark Musings__

The perfect companion piece to Light Musings – The dark side of Xtina Marie's poetry delves into intense emotions: heartache, loss, hurt, pain, rage, and a dangerous consuming love which can drive one insane. Dark Musings is not a collection!

The author returned to the centuries old practice of Narrative Poetry— the telling of a story through poetry.

If you believe you are brave enough to explore the savage emotions of the human heart; Dark Musings will test your mettle.

<u>Light Musings</u>

The perfect companion piece to Dark Musings – an intriguing mirror image of the darkness you have just read, but no less deep and soul stirring.

What a web she weaves. Light Musings is a poetic narrative—a story told through related poems. Xtina Marie is a master of this style. Known by her fans as the Dark Poet Princess.

This term of endearment came about as a result of the horror genre embracing her first book: Dark Musings which continues to garner stellar reviews.

Light Musings will not disappoint her loyal fans as darkness is present within these pages as well. However, this latest book will show a much larger audience that Xtina's poetry pulls out every feeling the reader has ever experienced—forcing them to feel with her protagonist. Light Musings shows us that love is made from darkness and light; something Xtina Marie explores like no one else.